Get Over It!

by

Kate McVeigh

Harrison House
Tulsa, Oklahoma

Unless otherwise indicated, all Scripture quotations are taken from the *King James Version* of the Bible.

Scripture quotations marked AMP are taken from *The Amplified Bible. Old Testament* copyright © 1965, 1987 by Zondervan Corporation, Grand Rapids, Michigan. *New Testament* copyright © 1958, 1987 by The Lockman Foundation, La Habra, California. Used by permission.

Scripture quotations marked NIV are taken from the *Holy Bible: New International Version* ® NIV ®. Copyright © 1973, 1978, 1984 by International Bible Society. Used by permission of Zondervan Publishing House. All rights reserved.

Direct quotations from the Bible appear in bold type.

Get Over It!
ISBN 1-57794-172-1

P.O. Box 690753
Tulsa, Oklahoma 74169

Published by Harrison House, Inc.
P.O. Box 35035
Tulsa, Oklahoma 74153

Contents

Offenses are the seeds from which unforgiveness develops and bitterness grows. The longer we hold onto unforgiveness over an offense, the more it affects our entire being: our personality, our attitude, our actions, our perspective and our relationships—especially our fellowship with God.

When someone has hurt or offended us, we often react just as if the person had stolen something from us. We tend to think that person owes us something. That's why Jesus taught us to pray, **...Forgive us our debts, as we forgive our debtors** (Matt. 6:12). Jesus also explained the reason why it's so important for us to forgive: **Whenever you stand praying, if you have anything against anyone, forgive him and let it drop...in order that your Father who is in heaven may also forgive you** (Mark 11:25 AMP). So, if you're carrying the weight of unforgiveness because someone has offended you, stop hindering your own progress. It's time to just get over it!

Kate McVeigh is a bright young woman diligently fulfilling God's call on her life by reaching as many people as possible for the Lord Jesus Christ. In her book, *Get Over It,* Kate shares simple yet life-changing examples of how you can let go of the weight of offense, move on and get over it! God wants you free to experience life to the fullest. And if you'll follow the path to freedom Kate outlines in this little book, your victory is assured.

Joyce Meyer

Introduction

As I travel all over the world ministering the gospel, I often see people who have been hurt by others and, for one reason or another, have been unable to put that hurt behind them.

Unresolved hurt hinders the person burdened by it from going out further in his walk with God. And because hurting people hurt other people, the one who has been hurt often may go on to wound others in the same way he has been wounded.

A person who has been hurt by someone else's actions has actually been *offended.* The dictionary defines an *offense* as an act that causes anger, resentment, displeasure or affront.[1]

It makes the devil happy when he can influence people to do things to offend other people. In fact, that's one of his main strategies against the body of Christ. He likes to use offense to separate and divide people from the very person or place that could possibly help them.

I encourage you as you read this book to examine your life. Do you find that you are easily angered or hurt by other people? Is it difficult for you to forgive someone who has offended you in some way? Well, God wants to set you free from *all* offense! This book is designed to help bring you to that place of freedom and victory in your spiritual walk.

My prayer for you is that you will experience the power of the Holy Spirit to overcome offenses in your life and be free once and for all.

Kate McVeigh

CHAPTER 1

Don't Miss Your Miracle!

God has all kinds of blessings and miracles reserved just for you. In fact, He has already made provision in His Word for every need you could ever possibly have in life.

But sometimes the miracles God has for us are left gathering dust on heaven's shelf. Why is that? Well, all too often it's our own fault. We allow our channel of communication with God to get clogged up with unforgiven offenses. And because we let resentment and unforgiveness fester inside of us unchecked, we end up missing our miracle.

So how do we make sure we *don't* miss the miracles God wants to perform in our lives? We find out how to deal with offenses according to the Word—and then we do it just that way!

You see, I can't promise you that you will ever get to a place in your spiritual walk where you won't have to deal with offenses. The Bible assures us that offenses *will* come to us in this life. In fact, in Matthew 18:7, Jesus Himself said, **For it must needs be that offences come.**

However, God wants us to be overcomers in *every* area of life, and that includes overcoming every offense that comes our way.

Offense Over Trivialities

I am continually amazed by the variety of reasons people give for leaving churches, jobs, families or other important life situations. These people become offended at the most trivial things. For example, one woman told me that she believed God had called her to attend a certain church—but then later she left because the music was too loud!

I asked this woman, "Why didn't you just sit in the back of the church or use earplugs rather than leave the church God told you to attend?" Well, this woman didn't have a good answer to give me! She was just doing what most people do—run when they become offended.

Don't let the devil do that to you. Don't let him run you out of your church, workplace or important relationships because of an offense. God wants you to walk in victory over offenses. He wants you to live completely free from the hurt and turmoil they can cause.

So if something has happened that has offended you, pray about your situation; then stand in faith in the midst of it and keep the devil from gaining the upper hand. Later, if God leads you out of that situation, you'll leave in victory instead of in hurt and offense.

The Devil's Trap of Offense

Let's talk a little more about what it means to be offended. Another dictionary definition of *offense* is "an act of stumbling; a cause or occasion of sin; a stumbling block."[1]

In the Bible, the word *offense* comes from the New Testament Greek word *skandalon*—the same Greek word that the English word *scandal* is derived from. That word *skandalon* refers to the part of a trap to which a bait is attached.[2] In other words, an offense is a trap the devil has baited to cause you to stumble and fall!

Someone may have done something *to* you or said something *about* you that caused you to be offended. You may feel hurt and misunderstood, or you may feel resentful and angry toward that person. But regardless of how that offense makes you feel, you will fall into the trap the devil has set for you if you don't make the decision to *let that offense go.* God has made a way in His Word for you to overcome offenses.

Scandal:
A Stumbling Block of Offense

One of the main traps of offense the devil likes to use is *scandalous gossip.* The truth is, it's hard to think of anything that works as efficiently as gossip to cause hurt and offense between two people.

Just think about the game "Telephone" that you used to play when you were a child. You would whisper a sentence in someone's ear; then that person would whisper whatever he heard into the ear of the next person.

This same process would continue around the circle of people who were playing the game. And by the time the last person heard what had been passed around the circle, it would be something entirely different than the original sentence!

Often it seems that scandal circulates just that way in the body of Christ.

Someone shares with another person a piece of information regarding another believer's personal life. Before you know it, what started out as a simple story has escalated into juicy gossip that no longer resembles the original account at all! And the person who is the source of discussion is the one who suffers.

The book of Proverbs has a lot to say about the dangers of gossip and scandal. Let's look at some of those Scriptures:

> **A gossip betrays a confidence, but a trustworthy man keeps a secret.**
>
> **Proverbs 11:13 NIV**

> **A perverse man stirs up dissension, and a gossip separates close friends.**
>
> **Proverbs 16:28 NIV**

> **A gossip betrays a confidence; so avoid a man who talks too much.**
>
> **Proverbs 20:19 NIV**

Without wood a fire goes out;
without gossip a quarrel dies down.
Proverbs 26:20 NIV

God is giving us a very clear message: As Christians, we must be very careful to avoid giving offense by repeating scandalous gossip.

A Trap To Distract You

If you allow yourself to focus on an offense you have suffered, it will become a trap that distracts you from doing what God would want you to do. The truth is, an unforgiven offense can hinder you from accomplishing God's will for your life.

When you become offended by something a person says to you or about you, your mind can become consumed and distracted by that offense if you're not careful. That's why Isaiah 26:3 says, **Thou wilt keep him in perfect peace, whose mind is stayed on thee.**

You see, the mind is where the real battle takes place. Therefore, in order for us to live full of peace and free from offense the way God intends, we have to continually focus our thoughts on God and His Word.

Second Corinthians 10:5 explains what we are to do with our thought life: **Casting down imaginations, and every high thing that exalteth itself against the knowledge of God, and bringing into captivity every thought to the obedience of Christ.** That means when an offense comes, it's our responsibility to take captive every thought about that offense, bringing it into obedience to the Head of the Church, Jesus Christ.

But all too often instead of taking our negative thoughts captive, we allow those thoughts to take *us* captive! We allow wrong imaginations to cast *us* down. It's time to put a stop to that. We need to take hold of all our resentful, angry thoughts and make them line up with the Word of God.

Reacting in the Natural

Most of us *want* to act in the Spirit according to the Word of God. But all too often we react in the natural, or in the flesh, taking offense over little things that people do or say.

Proverbs 18:19 paints a picture of a man who, when offended, reacts in the natural rather than in the Spirit: **A brother offended is harder to be won than a strong city: and their contentions are like the bars of a castle.**

When I read that verse, I think of the ancient castles I visited during a trip to Scotland. The castle dungeons are constructed with strong, heavy bars designed to keep prisoners in and everyone else out.

Well, the same thing can be true in the spiritual realm. When we get offended, we often put up invisible bars between ourselves and others, just like the bars in those castles. Those "bars of offense" serve the same purpose as the natural bars—they keep us hidden within ourselves, isolated from anyone who might hurt us.

Sometimes that kind of behavior is called "the silent treatment." We use our silence as a weapon to make sure those who have offended us know that they've messed up. We also use it to let everyone else know we've been offended.

But the silent treatment is just one example of reacting in the natural to an offense rather than walking in the love of God. The Bible says that real love **keeps no record of wrongs** (1 Corinthians 13:5 NIV).

Stamp Out Strife

In my ministry office, we have a code that we use to diffuse potentially offensive situations. We call it "SOS," which stands for "Stamp Out Strife." We are very aware that the Word says, **For where envying and strife**

is, there is confusion and every evil work (James 3:16).

So when we begin to get a little edgy and things start going wrong, one of us yells, "SOS! SOS!" That puts everyone else on immediate notice that strife is rearing its ugly head. It's time to stop talking, calm down and ask the Holy Spirit to help us walk in love in that situation. We have found this to be a very effective way to stamp out strife!

You can do the same thing. When things start going wrong in your life, get out your "SOS flag" and start waving it. Stamp out the strife! How? *By choosing to walk in the love of God.* Love never fails.

Avoid Those Who Cause Offense

Some people seem to major in offending others. Seldom a day goes by that they don't say or do something that cause offense to someone.

Determine not to be like those people. Romans 16:17 says, **Now I beseech you, brethren, mark them which cause divisions and offences contrary to the doctrine which ye have learned; *and avoid them.***

Notice that this verse *didn't* say, "Mark them which cause divisions and offenses and *talk about them.*" No, it says, *"Avoid* them." That means you can avoid certain problems by avoiding certain people.

Have you ever been around people who just seem to pull gossip out of you? Well, the Bible tells you what you can do about it: *Avoid them.*

First Peter 3:10 provides a key that will keep you from becoming like those people who make a practice of offending others:

> **For he that will love life, and see good days, *let him refrain his tongue***

***from the evil,* and his lips that they speak no guile.**

Do you want to see good days and live a long life free from offense? Then keep your tongue from evil, and speak good things about others!

Don't Fall Into the Devil's Trap

Remember—offenses are the devil's trap to stop you from fulfilling God's will for your life.

It isn't always easy to avoid those traps. For instance, when I was a teenager, I talked with a highly respected Christian about the fact that I felt God was calling me into the ministry. They told me that the Lord could not use me because I was a woman and I was not educated enough! If I had held on to that offense and had not begun to step out in the ministry I knew God was calling me to, I would have missed His perfect plan for my life. And do you know that many years later, I ministered in that same person's church, and I was told by them that I was one of the best ministers they had ever heard! I don't think they even remembered what they had said years before. So many times, you and I can be offended and the other person isn't even aware of what they did or said. They're not losing any sleep over it, so why should you?

Friend, I'm telling you—offenses are a deadly trap of the devil. So refuse to fall into that trap. Don't let offenses stop you from doing what God wants you to do!

The Lord Teaches Me a Lesson

One time I was visiting a church service, and the pastor asked all the ministers present to stand so he could recognize and welcome us to the meeting. Several of us stood, and he recognized each one of us individually.

A woman in a wheelchair was sitting in the row behind me and the other ministers I was sitting with. When the pastor asked for ministers to stand, she raised her hand. But the pastor didn't see her raised hand, so she wasn't recognized as a minister with the rest of us.

After we sat back down, the pastor just went on with the service. I thought, *Lord, I hope that woman didn't get offended!*

The Lord answered, "I'm going to teach you something." I had no idea what the Lord meant by that, so I decided to just sit back and listen to the sermon.

The guest minister began to preach. After about five minutes, he stopped his sermon. He looked at the woman in the wheelchair and asked her, "Do you have faith to get out of that wheelchair?"

The woman replied, "Yes, I do."

"Well, then," the minister said, *"Get up!"*

Instantly the woman got up and walked all over the building, completely healed. Until that moment, she hadn't walked in five years!

I spoke with the woman after the service and asked her if she had been offended when the pastor didn't acknowledge her. She said the devil had tried to make her feel rejected and unimportant. Then she told me she just made up her mind that she wasn't going to miss out on what God might have for her in that meeting over an offense. She realized that love doesn't have to be noticed.

That woman could have taken offense at the pastor's failure to acknowledge her and said to herself, *That pastor didn't recognize me as a minister. I'm offended!* But if she had done that, she might have missed her miracle!

Remember, God has miracles reserved just for you as well. Don't miss those miracles because of a silly little offense. *Refuse* to let the devil win as he tries to make you lose

the blessings God has for you through stumbling block of offense.

CHAPTER 2
Three Kinds of Offense

Now I want to show you three different kinds of offense that believers commonly face.

You see, all of us have been offended by someone at one time or another. And, of course, offense works both ways. I'm sure we have all been used by the enemy to offend someone else as well!

But we must get to the place in our spiritual walk where we not only refrain from offending others, but we overcome the offenses done to us.

Offenses Come Back to You

Why is this subject of overcoming offenses so crucial? Well, offenses are like boomerangs. As a child, I used to watch cartoons in which one of the cartoon characters would throw a boomerang into the distance and then walk away, thinking that the boomerang was gone forever. But then all of a sudden, it would come back and hit him on the head!

If you throw a boomerang the correct way, it will come back to you. It's the same way with offenses: When you offend another person, that offense will usually return to you in one form or another.

The reason it is so important not to offend others is because the Bible clearly tells us in Galatians 6:7 that "whatever we sow, we reap...." A good friend of mine, who is now a pastor's wife, shared with me that, back when she and her husband were associate pastors, on several occasions the people in the congregation would want to talk to them about the things they didn't like about the senior pastor. At first, they felt they were justified in "listening" and "helping out someone who was struggling," but later they learned they were wrong. Although they eventually learned not to engage in such talk and to encourage those who came to them to go directly to the pastor with whom they had offense, they hadn't always handled it that way. Now that they are pastors themselves, people on their staff have gotten involved in gossip about them! They now see the value of always believing the best in others and trying to put yourself in their shoes before you stand in judgment of them.

It doesn't matter whether you send out boomerangs of kindness or offense, they will always come back to you!

Offenses Will Come

Let's look again at what Jesus said about offenses in Matthew 18:7:

> **Woe unto the world because of offences! For it must needs be that offences come; but woe to that man by whom the offence cometh!**

Jesus tells us here that offenses *will* come our way. Isn't that exciting? No, most Christians don't consider that kind of news exciting at all! Nor do they rejoice when Jesus promises, **In the world ye shall have tribulation** (John 16:33). However, Jesus ends that statement with a note of comfort: **But be of good cheer; I have overcome the world.**

Offenses will come, but you can be an overcomer in every situation, no matter what anyone may do to you. God shows you in His Word how to let go of offense and walk in victory.

Offense Caused by Your Stand for God

First, let's talk about those times when other people become offended by your stand for God.

Have your friends or relatives ever taken offense because you took a firm stand to serve God, refusing to participate in sin any longer? This has happened to me. For example, although my brother has been saved for several years now, there was a time before he became a Christian that he would tease me about my "radical" stand for Jesus. He'd say things like, "Praise the Lord, Kate!" in a very sarcastic tone of voice.

My brother was trying to offend me—and he succeeded! To tell you the truth, sometimes I wanted to punch him and ask for forgiveness later. But I chose to let go of the offense and walk in love instead.

I told him, "The Bible says in Acts 16:31 that if I believe on the Lord Jesus Christ, I and my household will be saved. Mark my words—one day you're going to *really* praise the Lord with me!"

Well, a few years later my brother did get saved. Not long afterwards, I was preaching in his area, and he went to a service with me. As we stood next to each other during praise and worship, he lifted his hands high above his head, praising God. Then he nudged me and said earnestly, "Praise the Lord, Kate!" This time he really meant it! God is a good God!

As I witnessed the change Jesus made in my brother's life, I can't tell you how glad I was that I had decided to walk in love when he tried to offend me. I mean, what do you think would have happened if I had given him "the silent treatment," holding him off at arm's length with those invisible bars of unforgiveness? I'll tell you what could have happened: My brother might never have gotten saved.

There's no doubt about it—holding on to an offense is serious business!

Jesus also experienced this particular type of offense in His life and ministry. People were offended with His stand when He started to be used by God and stepped out into His ministry.

Those who lived in Jesus' hometown were amazed at the signs and wonders that followed Him. They asked, "Isn't that Joseph's son? Didn't our children play with Him? Who does He think He is?" They were offended that the little boy they had watched grow into manhood could now be so mightily used of God.

Jesus was even accused of operating under the devil's power. (And you thought someone told a lie about *you!)*

> **Then was brought unto him one possessed with a devil, blind, and dumb: and he healed him, insomuch that the blind and dumb both spake and saw. And all the people were amazed, and said, Is not this the son of David?**
>
> **But when the Pharisees heard it, they said, This fellow doth not cast out devils, but by Beelzebub the prince of the devils.**
>
> Matthew 12:22-24

Jesus could have become very offended when the Pharisees said this. He could have said, "Forget this! I'm tired of being falsely accused! I'm going back to heaven and leaving all of you join the devil in hell—good-bye!"

Aren't you glad Jesus didn't do that? He didn't operate in offense; He operated in the love of God.

God may be calling you to do something in life that is beyond the ordinary. Well, not everyone is going to appreciate your vision or back you 100 percent. However, it is not your job to pacify or satisfy all those who are offended by your stand for God. Your job is to walk in His love.

I like what one respected minister had to say on the subject. He maintained that if people accused him of killing his own grandma, he wouldn't even stop to deny it; he'd just let God fight his battles for him!

You see, you don't need to defend yourself when someone offends you. Just pray, walk in love and be led by the Holy Spirit. When you do your part, God will fight your battles for you!

Offended with God

A second type of offense occurs when people become offended with God Himself. Perhaps someone prayed about something, and it seemed to him that God didn't answer his prayer.

For example, I remember at one time in my life, there was a certain job that I really wanted. I prayed so hard that I would be hired, but I never got the job! I could have been offended with God, but looking back on the situation, I now thank Him that the prayer was not answered in the way that I had hoped, because now I can clearly see that it wasn't His will. God had something much better in store for me. Had I gotten that job, I would have missed out on countless blessings.

If you have never experienced this type of offense, someone you know probably has. Unfortunately, it's a very common problem among believers.

You see, Satan is the one sending those thoughts that place the blame on God. The devil *wants* us to take offense with Him. He knows that when we are offended with God, we are not walking close to Him. And that's exactly where the enemy wants us: out of fellowship with the Lord.

But we should never blame or become offended with God. He is our loving Father. He is on our side. In fact, He loved us so much that He actually sent His only Son to die for our sins!

If anyone has ever been lied about, it's God Himself. Even the world system blames God for a lot of things He never caused.

For example, when such things as storms, floods, earthquakes or volcanic eruptions cause immense damage, insurance companies call them "acts of God." But the truth is, those natural disasters are acts of destruction and death. They certainly don't come from the One Who is the Giver of life!

Offended by Our Own Shortcomings

A third type of offense occurs when people become offended with themselves because they keep falling short in a certain area of their lives.

Have you ever become offended with yourself? Maybe you got mad at yourself and thought, *I'm so tired of always blowing it in this same area!* In fact, you may have confessed First John 1:9 so much, you thought you wore that verse right out of the Bible. But you didn't!

Peter's experience after Jesus was crucified is a good example of this type of offense. Peter became offended with himself because he denied Jesus. He was the one who boasted,

"Lord, I'll never deny You! I'll love You to the end." Then Peter denied the Lord three times. (John 13:37,38; 18:17,25-27.)

Peter was mad at himself for blowing it. He was so discouraged, he decided to go back to his old trade of fishing. Some of the other disciples said, "We're going too." (John 21:3.)

The men were unsuccessful until the resurrected Jesus appeared the next morning on the beach and called to them, "Listen, men, cast your nets on the other side of the boat." When they obeyed Jesus' instructions, their nets overflowed with fish. (vv. 4-6.)

Peter had been so offended at himself and so confused by the events of the crucifixion that he decided his life was better before he became a disciple.

Many Christians feel that way at one time or another. When things get difficult in their Christian walk, they look back with longing to the past, thinking that what they did

before they met the Lord was better than what they are doing now. Of course, that line of thinking is nothing but a trick of the enemy designed to distract them from what God has called them to do.

Anyway, that's how Peter was feeling as he cast out to sea in his old fishing boat. So later, as Jesus and the disciples sat eating fish around the fire, Jesus ministered to Peter and delivered him of offense.

The happy ending to Peter's misery is found in John 21:15-19 NIV:

> **When they had finished eating, Jesus said to Simon Peter, "Simon son of John, do you truly love me more than these?" "Yes, Lord," he said, "you know that I love you." Jesus said, "Feed my lambs."**
>
> **Again Jesus said, "Simon son of John, do you truly love me?" He answered, "Yes, Lord, you know that I**

love you." Jesus said, "Take care of my sheep."

The third time he said to him, "Simon son of John, do you love me?" Peter was hurt because Jesus asked him the third time, "Do you love me?" He said, "Lord, you know all things; you know that I love you." Jesus said, "Feed my sheep. I tell you the truth, when you were younger you dressed yourself and went where you wanted; but when you are old you will stretch out your hands, and someone else will dress you and lead you where you do not want to go."

Jesus said this to indicate the kind of death by which Peter would glorify God. Then he said to him, "Follow me!"

In this passage of Scripture, Jesus delivered Peter from the offense he had committed when he denied Jesus three times. In fact, Jesus told him, "Peter, you are going to love Me so much, you're even going to be a martyr."

Never again do we see Peter operate out of offense in his ministry. Furthermore, he did not miss the ministry God had called him to fulfill.

You don't need to miss what God has for you either. Just let the Lord minister His forgiveness and love to you. He wants to set you free from the guilt and condemnation that come when you are offended with yourself.

Turn Away From Past Failures

So don't stay offended with yourself or anyone else. God wants you to walk in victory over offense. However, you can't effectively run forward into what God has called you to do while you're still looking back at the past.

I learned that lesson the hard way one day when I was a tomboy playing football with some other kids in the street. I went out for a pass, running just as fast as I

could—and when I looked back to catch the ball, I smashed right into a parked car. I guarantee you, I never did *that* again!

If you try to run forward in God while looking back at your past failures, you *will* get tripped up. There is no way you can keep holding on to the failures or offenses of the past and still effectively run the race God has set before you.

God wants to set you free from the hurts of the past. It doesn't matter what you've done, the word "past" means *past.*

Perhaps your "past" happened just five minutes ago. Ask God to heal you of any offense you have suffered and to forgive you for any wrong reaction to that offense. Then rest in the fact that God is faithful.

Stand fast on First John 1:9. This verse wasn't written to sinners; it was written to *believers.* John said, **If we confess our sins, he is faithful and just to forgive our sins, and to cleanse us from all unrighteousness.**

I heard that someone once conducted an analytical study of the word *all,* tracing it back to its roots. That person discovered that the word "all" literally means *all!*

The Bible says it is God **who forgiveth *all* thine iniquities; who healeth *all* thy diseases** (Psalm 103:3). In other words, God isn't holding the past against you. You need to forgive yourself of the past and let it go.

It doesn't matter how many times you have fallen short in an area, once you confess your sin, God does not remember it anymore. I heard a minister talk about how he was feeling condemned and guilty for blowing it again in the same area. He went before the Lord saying, "God, I must be coming to you for the 92nd time to ask for forgiveness for the same thing." The Lord replied, "To you it's the 92nd time, but to me it's the first time!" The Lord showed him that all those other times were forgotten because they were washed clean by the blood of Jesus! Now, that isn't an excuse for continual sin, but if you have missed it, there is forgiveness!

So keep yourself free from these three types of offense we have discussed. As you do, God will make sure you don't miss the ministry and the work He has called you to fulfill.

Therefore David ran, and stood upon the Philistine, and took his sword, and drew it out of the sheath thereof, and slew him, and cut off his head therewith. And when the Philistines saw their champion was dead, they fled.

1 Samuel 17:40,44,45,48,49,51

Now, do you think David would have
joyed that kind of success against Goliath
ie had decided to take offense earlier
en his brother mocked him? No way!
l was able to undertake on David's
alf to help him win the victory because
d's heart was right before Him.

David had gotten angry and bitter over
other's insults, he would not have
enced one of his greatest victories—a
that ultimately affected the course of
ire life. That's how dangerous it can
e in offense!

CHAPTER 3

Overcoming the Giants in Your Life

David is a prime example of someone who didn't allow himself to become offended. And because he didn't wallow in bitterness and offense, David was able to slay a giant and win the battle. (1 Samuel 17:1-51.)

Facing the Giant Goliath

When David was still just a teenager tending his family's sheep, his father sent him down to the battlefield where the Israelites and the Philistines were preparing to fight each other. (vv. 17,18.)

David's job was to take food to his brothers and check to see how they were doing. When he arrived at the battlefield, his oldest brother, Eliab, promptly gave him an opportunity to become offended.

When Eliab saw David talking to the other soldiers about the giant Goliath's challenge to fight, Eliab taunted David, saying, "You didn't come down here to bring us food—you just came here to watch the battle!" (v. 28.)

David could have taken offense right then. He could have run all the way home to his father and complained, "You're not going to believe this, Dad! Eliab embarrassed me in front of the whole army of Israel! He accused me of having wrong motives for going down there. I'm so mad at him!"

Instead, David let his brother's mocking words roll right off him. He stayed in the camp—and you know what happened next: Through his faith in God, David killed the giant Goliath!

> **And he [David] took his staff in his hand, and chose him five smooth stones out of the brook, and put them in a shepherd's bag which he**

> **had, even in a scrip; and his sling was in his hand: and he drew near t**
> **the Philistine....**
>
> **And the Philistine said to David**
> **Come to me, and I will give thy fl**
> **unto the fowls of the air, and to**
> **beasts of the field.**
>
> **Then said David to the Phili**
> **Thou comest to me with a swo**
> **with a spear, and with a shiel**
> **come to thee in the name of**
> **of hosts, the God of the arm**
> **Israel, whom thou hast def**
>
> **And it came to pass, wh**
> **Philistine arose, and cam**
> **nigh to meet David, that**
> **hasted, and ran toward**
> **meet the Philistine. An**
> **his hand in his bag, a**
> **a stone, and slang it,**
> **Philistine in his fore**
> **stone sunk into his**
> **fell upon his face**

en
if
wh
Go
beh
Dav

If
his b
exper
victory
his ent
be to li

Offense Short-Circuits God's Power

I know there are "giants" in your life that God wants you to kill. For example, you may be facing a financial giant or a giant of sickness and disease in your life. Perhaps your children aren't serving the Lord. These and many other problems can seem like huge giants in your life that require great faith to overcome.

But you won't be able to effectively overcome your giant if you continue to hold on to offenses. Unforgiveness—which is the opposite of walking in love— will stop the power of God from flowing to you and through you. Galatians 5:6 explains why this is so: **For in Jesus Christ neither circumcision availeth any thing, nor uncircumcision; but *faith which worketh by love.***

God gave us His Word so we would have a way out of every offensive situation that could steal victory from our lives. Jesus tells us in John 16:1, **These things have I spoken unto you, *that ye should not be offended.***

God has given us the ability and the means to stand in faith on His Word, to walk in love and to avoid being taken in by offenses. But it's still up to us to *use* what He's given us. We have to absolutely refuse to hold on to offenses so we can be free to slay the giants in our lives!

A Mother's Plight

In Mark 7, we find the account of a woman who overcame a huge giant in her life because she refused to take offense. This woman's daughter was vexed by a devil.

Now, think about that particular giant. If your daughter had a devil, you'd have trouble, wouldn't you?

This desperate mother went to Jesus looking for help. But when she heard what Jesus had to say to her, she had to make a choice: to receive what He said in humility and faith, or to take offense and miss the miracle God had for her.

This is the woman's story:

> **For a certain woman, whose young daughter had an unclean spirit, heard of him, and came and fell at his feet: The woman was a Greek, a Syrophenician by nation; and she besought him that he would cast forth the devil out of her daughter.**
>
> **But Jesus said unto her, Let the children first be filled: for it is not meet to take the children's bread, and to cast it unto the dogs.**
>
> Mark 7:25-27

When Jesus said to this woman, **It is not meet to take the children's bread, and to cast it unto the dogs,** she could have taken offense and said indignantly, "Jesus called me a dog!" She could have told her daughter,

"Come on, Honey, let's get out of here! Did you hear what He called us?"

But if the woman had done that, she would have missed the miracle God had planned for her daughter's life, and the giant she was facing would never have been overcome.

Thank God, the Syrophoenician woman did *not* become offended. Instead, she responded with humility:

> **And she answered and said unto him, Yes, Lord: yet the dogs under the table eat of the children's crumbs.**
>
> **And he said unto her, For this saying go thy way; *the devil is gone out of thy daughter.***
>
> **Mark 7:28,29**

Healing came to that little girl! Deliverance came and set her free! Why? Because that desperate mother humbled herself before the Lord and *did not get offended!*

Fear of What Others Think Can Lead to Offense

So follow that mother's example, and don't allow yourself to become stuck in the trap of constantly worrying about what people think or say about you. Proverbs 29:25 says that **the fear of man bringeth a snare**—a snare that often comes in the form of an offense.

If you are ensnared by a fear of people, you will only be able to go so far in God before you get jerked back by that snare, just as a leash limits a dog's reach. For instance, someone may say something negative about you that hurts or offends you. As a result of what that person says about you, you may choose to pull back from doing what God has called you to do.

Personally, I don't want to be limited in my life by a fear of people. I want to go all the way in God. I want to do *all* that God has called me to do. How about you?

A Brother's Forgiveness

Now let's look at the account of Jephthah in Judges 11. Jephthah was asked to face a big "giant"—the mighty Ammonite army. This story shows how his correct response to an offense caused by his own brothers helped lead him to victory.

> **Now Jephthah the Gileadite was a mighty man of valour, and he was the son of a harlot: and Gilead begat Jephthah. And Gilead's wife bare him sons; and his wife's sons grew up, and they thrust out Jephthah, and said unto him, Thou shalt not inherit in our father's house; for thou art the son of a strange woman.**
>
> **Judges 11:1,2**

Did you notice that the Bible calls Jephthah a mighty man of valor? He was a great warrior, but his half brothers got mad at him and kicked him out of the house. They told Jephthah, "You're not going to receive your part of the inheritance. We're keeping it!"

This was definitely an opportunity for Jephthah to take offense. People can really get offended over issues of money, and Jephthah certainly did in this situation. After all, he was cheated out of his inheritance!

If you go on reading, you'll find that Jephthah fled to the land of Tob. During the time that he was there, the Ammonites went to war against Israel. (vv. 3,4). His brothers knew they would never survive without his help. So when trouble came knocking at their door, guess who they called on? Jephthah. (Have you ever been offended by someone who later called you for help the minute trouble came his way?)

Jephthah could have told his scheming brothers, "You guys kicked me out and then kept my inheritance. If you think I'm going to help you, you're crazy!"

But Jephthah didn't respond that way. He walked in love. He returned home and helped his brothers win the battle. (vv. 21,22.)

Verse 29 goes on to say, **Then the Spirit of the Lord came upon Jephthah.** In other words, Jephthah didn't give in to his offense. Winning the battle was more important to him than that offense—and as a result of walking in love, the Spirit of the Lord came upon him.

Like Jephthah, you may have been offended by someone in the past. But you can adopt Jephthah's attitude of forgetting every offense and concentrating instead on winning the victory over the giants in your life. And as you walk in the love of God, the Holy Spirit will enable you to win every battle you're facing!

How To Have a Conscience Free From Offense

We can learn a lot about this subject of overcoming offense by looking at the life of the apostle Paul. Paul was one of the greatest examples in the Bible of someone who lived free from offense.

If anyone ever had the opportunity to be offended at God and man, it would have been Paul. He was beaten, shipwrecked, robbed, stoned, hated and lied about. In fact, just about any form of persecution you can imagine, Paul endured. (2 Corinthians 11:23-28.)

However, after experiencing all these troubles, Paul was still able to say, **And herein do I exercise myself, to have always a conscience void of offense toward God, and toward men** (Acts 24:16).

Paul made it clear that a person can't become free from offense overnight. He said, **I *exercise* myself.** In other words, it's *work* to maintain a conscience void of offense toward God and man!

Think about what it takes to see any benefit from exercise. For instance, you don't go down to the gym, perform one sit-up and then return home and say, "Whew! I really worked out today—I did one sit-up! I know I'll have great results!" No, you know that in order to see results from exercise, you have to do it countless times.

In the same way, you must constantly work to stay in the love of God and to keep yourself from getting offended by what people say or do to you. Only as you continually put the Word of God to work in your life can you maintain a conscience free from offense and overcome the giants you face.

Let me give you one example of how you can "exercise yourself" in this area as Paul did. Whenever an offensive situation arises, ask yourself these questions: *What does the Bible say about it?* and *What would Jesus do about it?* If you will automatically respond to every potentially offensive situation with these two questions, you will learn to stay free from all offenses.

In Matthew 11:6, Jesus gives us another clue to help maintain a conscience void of offense. He tells us: **And blessed is he, whosoever shall not be offended in me.**

How do we stay free from offense? By keeping ourselves *in Jesus.* When we abide in Jesus, we are free to love people, no matter what they may do to us.

When we operate on our own apart from Jesus, we soon find ourselves out of spiritual fuel, sputtering like a car that is out of gas. Suddenly we are more irritable than we ought to be. People grate on our nerves more than they normally do.

On the other hand, when we feed on the Word and maintain unbroken fellowship with Jesus, things that used to bother us greatly don't bother us quite as much anymore. That's why it's so important to abide in the Vine—Jesus Christ. (John 15:4.)

The Secret of Perfect Peace

What we are really talking about here is the key to living continually in the peace of God.

Peace is something the world is searching for desperately. In fact, if someone figured out a way to put peace in a bottle and sell it, he would be rich. But even though the people of the world are looking for peace, they are looking in all the wrong places.

Psalm 119:165 tells us the right place to look for peace: **Great peace have they *which love thy law.***

Do you want to enjoy God's supernatural peace, regardless of what happens to you? Then begin to love and meditate on the Word of God. As you do, great peace will come and fill your mind, your heart and every area of your life.

God said He will keep you in perfect peace as you keep your mind *stayed* or

But they often ask the question, "Just *how* do I go about forgiving those who have done so much to hurt me?"

We're going to find out from the Word of God some keys to operating in forgiveness. But first, we must realize that many times the reason people hurt us is that they have unresolved hurts of their own. The anger of someone who is lashing out at us may very well be a direct reflection of that person's own insecurities and problems.

Know Your Enemy

It is also very important for us to know o our real enemy is. Ephesians 6:12 iden- s the enemy:

For we wrestle not against flesh d blood, but against principalities, ainst powers, against the rulers of darkness of this world, against ritual wickedness in high places.

focused on Him. (Isaiah 26:3.) Your part is to keep your mind focused on God and His Word; God's part is to guarantee perfect peace in your life—and He is always faithful to perform what He promises!

Psalm 119:165 concludes by saying, ***Nothing* shall offend them.** As we begin to operate in and stand upon the Word of God, we will remain free from offenses. Nothing—and no one—will be able to offend us!

So get a vision of the victory that is possible for you to attain. You *can* overcome the giants in your life. You *can* live free from offenses. Remember, you have the love of God inside of you—a supernatural love that doesn't keep a record of suffered wrongs.

As you determine to walk in love, you will rise above the offenses that come your way. No matter what people say or do, God's peace will rule your heart because love never fails!

CHAPTER 4
Learn To Forgive

We have all experienced hurt in our lives in one way or another. I want to focus in this chapter on how we can ov come the emotional wounds caused by someone who has wronged us.

Of course, we know that we must fo those who have offended and hurt us, tells us in Mark 11:25 AMP that if we our prayers to be answered, we mus those who have hurt us:

> **And whenever you stand pr you have anything against ar forgive him and let it drop let it go), in order that you Who is in heaven may als you your [own] failings comings and let them d**

Most Christians know to forgive those who ha

wh
tifi
ar
ag
the
spi

We must recognize that although a *person* hurt us, Satan is ultimately the one behind the attack. The devil uses people to discourage us through offense.

Matthew 16 gives us a great illustration of a time the devil used Peter to try to discourage Jesus. Peter said the wrong thing at the wrong time. But Jesus recognized the demonic source behind the potential offense and stopped the devil in his tracks!

> **From that time forth Jesus began [clearly] to show His disciples that He must go to Jerusalem and suffer many things at the hands of the elders and the high priests and scribes, and be killed, and on the third day be raised from death.**
>
> **Then Peter took Him aside to speak to Him privately and began to reprove and charge Him sharply, saying, God forbid, Lord! This must never happen to You!**

But Jesus turned away from Peter and said to him, Get behind Me, Satan! You are in My way [an offense and a hindrance and a snare to Me]; for you are minding what partakes not of the nature and quality of God, but of men.

Matthew 16:21-23 AMP

We see here that Jesus was sharing with the disciples about going to the cross. Just then, Peter opened his big mouth and said the wrong thing: **Be it far from thee, Lord: this shall not be unto thee** (v. 22). If you look up that phrase in the original Hebrew, it literally means, "Pity Thyself, Lord." In other words, Peter was telling Jesus that He should feel sorry for Himself.

Of course, the thought of dying on the cross would tend to tempt anyone to feel sorry for himself. However, Jesus saw right through the whole thing. He didn't fall for the devil's trap; He knew what to do!

How did Jesus get rid of the discouragement that tried to latch onto Him? He spoke to it! He rebuked the temptation to be hurt, offended or filled with self-pity. Jesus resisted the real enemy, saying, **Get thee behind me, Satan** (v. 23).

Remember, an offense is a trap of the devil to cause you to fall. When discouragement comes, act just like Jesus and do exactly what He did—rebuke it! Notice that I said to rebuke *it,* not *the person who offended you.* Jesus rebuked the devil, *not* Peter.

If you have ever been hurt, you know that sometimes you are tempted to feel sorry for yourself. But don't give in to the devil. Get up and exercise your authority over him in the name of Jesus, boldly speaking forth the Word of God!

Let It Go

Notice what the scripture in Mark 11:25 AMP says to do with the offense: **Let it drop**

(leave it, let it go). Once we have forgiven someone, we are to let go of the offense.

You see, forgiveness is a *decision,* not a *feeling.* We can choose to forgive someone by faith in the same way we receive any of God's blessings.

So how do we let go of an offense? Well, for one thing, we stop talking about whatever has offended us.

Have you ever noticed that the more we talk about something, the bigger it gets? Even if it was years ago that something hurtful happened to us, we can cause the hurt to resurface all over again by retelling the same sad story one more time to someone else. We must learn to let go of the offense once and for all.

Another thing we can do to truly forgive someone and let go of the offense they have caused us is to realize that forgiveness is a free gift given to those who don't deserve it. That really shouldn't be too hard for us to understand. I mean, all we have to do is think about how much the Lord has already forgiven *us,* even when we didn't deserve it!

Keys to Forgiving

One thing I really like about Jesus is that He never tells you to do something you cannot do. If He did, He would be unjust, and God is a just and faithful God!

Not only did Jesus tell us to forgive, but He also shows us *how* to forgive. Let's take a look at four keys to releasing true forgiveness that Jesus gave us. These keys are all found in Matthew 5:44:

> **But I say unto you, *Love* your enemies, *bless* them that curse you, *do good* to them that hate you, and *pray* for them which despitefully use you, and persecute you.**

Key #1: Love

First of all, Jesus said to *love your enemies.* You are able to do that because the love of

God has been shed abroad in your heart by the Holy Ghost. (Romans 5:5.) By faith, you can say, "Lord, I love so-and-so and choose to forgive him (or her) in Jesus' name."

One thing that has helped me grow in love is to regularly meditate on the *Amplified Version* of First Corinthians 13:4-8:

> **Love endures long and is patient and kind; love never is envious nor boils over with jealousy, is not boastful or vainglorious, does not display itself haughtily.**
>
> **It is not conceited (arrogant and inflated with pride); it is not rude (unmannerly) and does not act unbecomingly. Love (God's love in us) does not insist on its own rights or its own way, for it is not self-seeking; it is not touchy or fretful or resentful; it takes no account of the evil done to it [it pays no attention to a suffered wrong]. It does not rejoice at**

injustice and unrighteousness, but rejoices when right and truth prevail.

Love bears up under anything and everything that comes, is ever ready to believe the best of every person, its hopes are fadeless under all circumstances, and it endures everything without weakening]. Love never fails [never fades out or becomes obsolete or comes to an end].

Wherever this passage of Scripture says *love,* we can insert our name there and apply its truth personally to our lives. For example, I can say, "*Kate* is not touchy or fretful or resentful; *Kate* takes no account of the evil done to her," etc. We can truthfully say this because the love of God resides within us.

Key #2: Bless

The second thing Jesus told us to do in Matthew 5:44 concerning those who have hurt us is to *bless them.*

The word *bless* in the Hebrew means "to speak well of."[1] Every time the devil reminds you of the people who have hurt you, just make a practice of saying, "Lord, bless them abundantly." Say something positive about them. Confess God's promises of blessing over them.

For instance, you could say, "The Holy Spirit is at work in so-and-so's life right now to teach him His ways. All hindrances are being removed from his life so he can be blessed going in and coming out!"

I know this isn't always easy, but Jesus wouldn't tell you to do something that you couldn't do.

Key #3: Do Good

This particular key is probably the most difficult one of all to act on: Jesus tells us to *do good to those who despitefully use us and persecute us.*

I want to encourage you to be led by the Holy Spirit in regard to this biblical command. I realize that in some extreme cases, it is best to have no contact with the one who has hurt you. But in most cases, you can do something good in the natural for that person according to the law of love.

Years ago I heard a testimony that a great woman of God related along these lines. The testimony blessed me so much that I want to share it with you. I believe it will bless you too!

This woman minister told about a time when a man (another minister) was really persecuting her ministry. The woman had a daily radio broadcast, so this story caught my attention! Each day after her broadcast, this man would come on the radio and say terrible things about her and her ministry.

This went on for quite some time. Needless to say, it started to bother the woman minister and raise questions in the minds of some of her listeners. But she decided to forgive the man, just as Jesus had said to do in Matthew 5:44. She prayed for the minister and blessed him according to this Scripture.

When she came to the part where Jesus said to do good to those who hate you and persecute you, she had a battle with her flesh. However, she put her flesh under and acted on the Word. She thought, *What can I do for this man that would be good?*

Well, if there is one thing any minister on the radio can use, it's money to pay for air time. So this woman minister decided to receive a special offering for him at her home church. She blessed him with a very good offering and a letter stating that she was praying for him and his ministry.

Guess what happened? The man repented! He told her how much the offering blessed him and asked her to forgive him. The next time he was on the radio, he apologized to all his listeners for what he had said about this woman minister. The Lord blessed these two ministers both in such a wonderful way through this entire situation that to this day, they are very close friends.

That's the power of walking in love instead of taking offense! So, if I have offended you in any way while you have been reading this book, send me a special offering—HA!

Key #4: Pray

The final key found in Matthew 5:44 is to *pray for those who have wronged us.* In fact, the best way you can truly forgive your enemies is to pray for them.

I learned this early in my Christian walk. You see, when I was first saved, I was so on fire for the Lord that I witnessed to everyone in my high school who would listen. I wanted everyone to get saved.

Everyone, that is, except for one person. There was a girl in my school who had caused me great hurt and pain in the past. To be very honest with you, I didn't care if she ever got saved! You can see that I really needed to forgive this girl.

My mother knew I was holding bitterness in my heart toward this girl. So Mom told me about a book she had read by Oral Roberts that greatly changed a similar situation she had once gone through.

In his book, Oral Roberts talked about forgiveness and praying for one's enemies. My mom related to me one important key that Brother Roberts stressed: If a person prays for his enemies, his feelings will eventually line up with the love of God in his heart.

So I decided to follow Brother Roberts' advice and pray for this girl every day. It wasn't long before I began to feel a real love for her. I knew in my heart that I had truly forgiven her.

Then one day, not long after I started praying for this girl, she showed up at my house. It was definitely a surprise to see her standing on my front porch!

The girl said to me, "I just happened to be in your neighborhood and wanted to ask you a question. Kate, what has happened to you? You've really changed."

"I asked Jesus to be my Savior," I replied. "Jesus opened my eyes and filled me with His love."

I began to share with her how she could experience the same life-changing peace through a personal relationship with Jesus. That afternoon I was able to pray with that girl who had hurt me so much in the past. She was gloriously saved and filled with the Holy Ghost right there in my house!

The girl also told me that she had a problem with her knee that was going to require surgery. So I laid hands on her to pray, and the power of God hit her so hard that she fell to the floor. When she got up, she was totally healed!

You see, when you pray for someone who has hurt you, you open the door for the Lord to do something great in your behalf. You have chosen to go love's way—God's higher way—and that causes you to rise above offenses until they have no more power to affect your life.

Become More Than a Conqueror Over Offense

Learning how to live free from offense is simply a part of growing up in God and becoming a mature Christian. By the power of the Holy Spirit living inside of you, you *can* walk in victory over offenses.

How can we be so sure of that? Because we know beyond a shadow of a doubt that First John 4:4 is true: **Greater is he that is in you, than he that is in the world.**

I encourage you to make the decision that from this day forward, you will *not* miss out on even one of the miracles God has for you because of unforgiveness in your heart. Walk in the love of God; live in His peace—and become more than a conqueror over the enemy's strategy of offense!

Five Tips To Help Overcome an Offense

1. Give the person who has caused the offense the benefit of the doubt. He or she may have just been having a bad day.

2. Remember, hurting people hurt people. There is a good chance that if someone is hurting you, he or she is hurting as well.

3. Keep in mind that your interpretation of a situation may be different than that of the person who offended you. He or she may not have meant it the way you took it.

4. Watch what you're continually thinking about. Do your best to keep your mind focused on the Lord at all times. (Isaiah 26:3.)

5. Pray about the situation. Cast the care of it over on the Lord; then don't worry about it anymore. (1 Peter 5:7.)

Seven Ways To Help You Stay Free From Offense

1. Love the person who has offended you. You can do it because God's love is in you. (Romans 5:5.)
2. Proclaim blessings over those who have offended you. (Matthew 5:44.)
3. Do something good for the person who has offended you. (Matthew 5:44.)
4. Earnestly pray for the well-being of the person who has caused the offense. (Matthew 5:44.)
5. Keep yourself built up in the Word of God. (Psalm 119:105.)
6. Spend time praying in the Spirit; it will help you stay in love. (Jude 1:20,21.)
7. Rely on the Holy Ghost; He's your Comforter and Helper. (John 14:16,17.)

Scripture References

25 AMP	Matthew 5:44
9 AMP	James 1:19 AMP
s 4:30-32	

To Live Free From Offense

Father, I thank You that Your love is shed abroad in my heart. Because I walk in Your love in every situation, I am not touchy or fretful or resentful. I take no account of the evil done to me, and I pay no attention to a suffered wrong. In fact, I am ever ready to believe the best of every person!

This day I exercise and discipline myself to keep a clear, unshaken conscience, void of offense toward God and man. I follow peace with all men and refuse to let a root of bitterness lodge within my heart through unforgiveness.

I bring every thought into captivity to the obedience of Christ and dwell only on that which is praiseworthy, honest and true. Therefore, I live in perfect peace as I keep my mind focused on God.

I will avoid offense in all that I do or say today; instead, my words and actions will be to the glory of God. As far as is possible with me, I will live peacably with everyone who crosses my path!

Scripture References

1 Corinthians 13:5,7 AMP	Acts 24:16 AMP
Hebrews 12:14,15	2 Corinthians 10:4,5
Philippians 4:8	Isaiah 26:3
1 Corinthians 10:31,32	Romans 12:18

Prayer T

Father, I purpc
have hurt or
every offense they
I give up any reser
them. In fact, I ask
every way today. I
happiness and prc

And because I f
failed me in some
You also forgive n
shortcomings so t
hindered.

Lord, in any sit
help me to be qu
person's side of t
offense and get a
I put away all bit
speaking and I fc
me, even as You
forgiven me. In J

Mar

1 Pe

Eph

Endnotes

Introduction

[1] *Webster's New World College Dictionary.* Macmillan: New York, 1996, p. 940, "offense."

Chapter One

[1] *Webster's New World College Dictionary.* Macmillan: New York, 1996, p. 940, "offense."

[2] James Strong, *Strong's Greek Dictionary of the New Testament.* Hendrickson: Peabody, MA, n.d., p. 65, #4625.

Chapter Four

[1] James Strong, *Strong's Hebrew and Chaldee Dictionary.* Hendrickson: Peabody, MA, n.d., p. 24, #1288.

If it be possible, as much as lieth in you, live peacably with all men.

Romans 12:18

Follow peace with all men and holiness, without which no man shall see the Lord: Looking diligently lest any man fail of the grace of God; lest any root of bitterness springing up trouble you, and thereby many be defiled.

Hebrews 12:14,15

And grieve not the holy Spirit of God, whereby ye are sealed unto the day of redemption.

Let all bitterness, and wrath, and anger, and clamour, and evil speaking, be put away from you, with all malice: And be ye kind one to another, tenderhearted, forgiving one another, even as God for Christ's sake hath forgiven you.

Ephesians 4:30-32

We put no obstruction in anybody's way [we give no offense in anything], so that no fault may be found and [our] ministry blamed and discredited.

2 Corinthians 6:3 AMP

Give none offence, neither to the Jews, nor to the Gentiles, nor to the church of God: Even as I please all men in all things, not seeking mine own profit, but the profit of many, that they may be saved.

1 Corinthians 10:32,33

And this I pray, that your love may abound yet more and more in knowledge and in all judgment; that ye may approve things that are excellent; that ye may be sincere and without offence till the day of Christ; being filled with the fruits of righteousness, which are by Jesus Christ, unto the glory and praise of God.

Philippians 1:9-11

Love endures long and is patient and kind; love never is envious nor boils over with jealousy, is not boastful or vainglorious, does not display itself haughtily.

It is not conceited (arrogant and inflated with pride); it is not rude (unmannerly) and does not act unbecomingly. Love (God's love in us) does not insist on its own rights or its own way, for it is not self-seeking; it is not touchy or fretful or resentful; it takes no account of the evil done to it [it pays no attention to a suffered wrong]. It does not rejoice at injustice and unrighteousness, but rejoices when right and truth prevail.

Love bears up under anything and everything that comes, is ever ready to believe the best of every person, its hopes are fadeless under all circumstances, and it endures everything [without weakening]. Love never fails [never fades out or becomes obsolete or comes to an end].

1 Corinthians 13:4-8 AMP

Therefore I always exercise and discipline myself [mortifying my body, deadening my carnal affections, bodily appetites, and worldly desires, endeavoring in all respects] to have a clear (unshaken, blameless) conscience, void of offense toward God and toward men.

Acts 24:16 AMP

Whether therefore ye eat, or drink, or whatsoever ye do, do all to the glory of God. Give none offence, neither to the Jews, nor to the Gentiles, nor to the church of God.

1 Corinthians 10:31,32

Understand [this], my beloved brethren. Let every man be quick to hear [a ready listener], slow to speak, slow to take offense and to get angry. For man's anger does not promote the righteousness God [wishes and requires].

James 1:19,20 AMP

Confess to one another therefore your faults (your slips, your false steps, your offenses, your sins) and pray [also] for one another, that you may be healed and restored [to a spiritual tone of mind and heart]. The earnest (heartfelt, continued) prayer of a righteous man makes tremendous power available [dynamic in its working].

James 5:16 AMP

When angry, do not sin; do not ever let your wrath (your exasperation, your fury or indignation) last until the sun goes down.

Ephesians 4:26 AMP

(For the weapons of our warfare are not carnal, but mighty through God to the pulling down of strong holds;) Casting down imaginations, and every high thing that exalteth itself against the knowledge of God, and bringing into captivity every thought to the obedience of Christ.

2 Corinthians 10:4,5

Finally, brethren, whatsoever things are true, whatsoever things are honest, whatsoever things are just, whatsoever things are pure, whatsoever things are lovely, whatsoever things are of good report; if there be any virtue, and if there be any praise, think on these things.

Philippians 4:8

But I say unto you, That whosoever is angry with his brother without a cause shall be in danger of the judgment: and whosoever shall say to his brother, Raca, shall be in danger of the council: but whosoever shall say, Thou fool, shall be in danger of hell fire.

Therefore if thou bring thy gift to the altar, and there rememberest that thy brother hath ought against thee; leave there thy gift before the altar, and go thy way; first be reconciled to thy brother, and then come and offer thy gift.

Matthew 5:22-24

But I say unto you, Love your enemies, bless them that curse you, do good to them that hate you, and pray for them which despitefully use you, and persecute you; that ye may be the children of your Father which is in heaven: for he maketh his sun to rise on the evil and on the good, and sendeth rain on the just and on the unjust.

Matthew 5:44,45

Never return evil for evil or insult for insult (scolding, tongue-lashing, berating), but on the contrary blessing [praying for their welfare, happiness, and protection, and truly pitying and loving them]. For know that to this you have been called, that you may yourselves inherit a blessing [from God—that you may obtain a blessing as heirs, bringing welfare and happiness and protection].

1 Peter 3:9 AMP

And whenever you stand praying, if you have anything against anyone, forgive him and let it drop (leave it, let it go), in order that your Father Who is in heaven may also forgive you your [own] failings and shortcomings and let them drop.

Mark 11:25 AMP

And blessed (happy, fortunate, and to be envied) is he who takes no offense at Me and finds no cause for stumbling in or through Me and is not hindered from seeing the Truth.

Matthew 11:6 AMP

Fathers, do not irritate and provoke your children to anger [do not exasperate them to resentment], but rear them [tenderly] in the training and discipline and the counsel and admonition of the Lord.

Ephesians 6:4 AMP

Now I beseech you, brethren, mark them which cause divisions and offences contrary to the doctrine which ye have learned; and avoid them.

Romans 16:17

For he that will love life, and see good days, let him refrain his tongue from evil, and his lips that they speak no guile: Let him eschew evil, and do good; let him seek peace, and ensue it.

1 Peter 3:10,11

If we confess our sins, he is faithful and just to forgive us our sins, and to cleanse us from all unrighteousness.

1 John 1:9

Hatred stirs up contentions, but love covers all transgressions.

Proverbs 10:12 AMP

A fool shows his annoyance at once, but a prudent man overlooks an insult.

Proverbs 12:16 NIV

A patient man has great understanding, but a quick-tempered man displays folly.

Proverbs 14:29 NIV

A hot-tempered man stirs up strife, but he who is slow to anger appeases contention.

Proverbs 15:18 AMP

Where no wood is, there the fire goeth out: so where there is no talebearer, the strife ceaseth.

Proverbs 26:20

The fear of man bringeth a snare: but whoso putteth his trust in the Lord shall be safe.

Proverbs 29:25

I have told you all these things, so that you should not be offended (taken unawares and falter, or be caused to stumble and fall away). [I told you to keep you from being scandalized and repelled.]

John 16:1 AMP

Great peace have they who love Your law; nothing shall offend them or make them stumble.

Psalm 119:165 AMP

Thou wilt keep him in perfect peace, whose mind is stayed on thee: because he trusteth in thee.

Isaiah 26:3

Prayer for Salvation

God cares for you and wants to help you overcome in every area of your life. That's why He sent Jesus to die for you.

If you have never received Jesus Christ as your personal Savior, you can make your heart right with God this very moment. In doing so, you will make heaven your eternal home.

Pray this prayer from your heart:

> *O God, I ask You to forgive me of my sins. I believe You sent Jesus to die on the cross for me. I receive Jesus Christ as my personal Savior. I confess Him as Lord of my life, and I give my life to Him. Thank You, Lord, for saving me and for making me new. In Jesus' name, amen.*

If you prayed this prayer for the first time, I want to welcome you to the family of God! Please write me at the address on the following page and let me know about your decision for Jesus. I'd like to send you some free literature to help you in your walk with the Lord.

For Further Information

To receive:

- additional copies of this book,
- a complete catalog of Rev. Kate McVeigh's books and tapes,
- a free subscription to her bimonthly newsletter or
- information regarding Kate's ministry schedule,

please write or call:

Kate McVeigh Ministries
P.O. Box 690753
Tulsa, Oklahoma 74169-0753
1-800-40-FAITH (1-800-403-2484)

Please include your prayer requests and comments when you write.

Additional copies of this book are available from your local bookstore.

HARRISON HOUSE
Tulsa, Oklahoma 74153

Power-Packed Teaching Materials

By Kate McVeigh

Audiotapes

"Walking in the Spirit" Series

The subjects discussed in this series are vital to your spiritual health!

You will learn:

- How to overcome the flesh.
- How to get rid of bad habits.
- The rewards of self-discipline.
- How diligence produces results.

4 tapes—$20.00

"Your Faith Will Make You Whole" Series

Without faith, it's impossible to enjoy the abundant life God has for you. This dynamic series teaches you:

- How to receive your healing or miracle from God.
- How your faith can make you whole in any area of life.
- How to catch the Spirit of faith.
- The principles of faith described in God's Word.

4 tapes—$20.00

"Having Victory Over Intimidation, Insecurity, Worry and Fear" Series

You can learn how to walk in victory over the intimidation, insecurity and fear the devil tries to send your way! In this series, Kate also discusses:

- How to live in boldness.
- Overcoming insecurities.
- How to walk in the freedom to be yourself!

4 tapes—$20.00

"Effective Prayer" Series

Learn how to receive an answer every time you pray! Titles in this series include:

- Seven Steps to Answered Prayer
- The Lord's Prayer
- How To Pray Effectively for Others
- Ask and You Shall Receive

4 tapes—$20.00

"God's Laws of Financial Increase" Series

If you struggle in the area of finances, this powerful six-tape series is for you! Kate teaches you:

- How to increase financially.
- God's plan of prosperity for your life.

6 tapes—$30.00

Books

The Favor Factor

In this book, Kate provides rich teaching on the subject of supernatural favor. You'll find out:

- What divine favor really is.
- How to release your faith for supernatural favor with God and man.
- Twenty ways to lose favor.
- Prayers for favor in various areas of life.

$7.00 each

The Doctrine of Healing

This helpful minibook contains:

- Healing scriptures.
- Reasons why God wants you healed.
- Cases of healing in the Bible.

$1.00 each

Presenting the Ministry of...

KATE MCVEIGH

Rev. Kate McVeigh travels extensively throughout the United States and abroad, boldly preaching the Gospel of Jesus Christ with signs and wonders following. Besides being an author, she also has many cassette teaching tapes in circulation. In addition, Kate's daily radio broadcase, "The Voice of Faith," airs throughout the United States.

Kate is known as a solid evangelist and teacher of the Gospel with an emphasis on healing the sick and winning the lost. Through Kate's down-to-earth and often humorous teaching of the Word, many people have been saved, healed and encouraged to attain God's highest for their lives.

The Harrison House Vision

Proclaiming the truth and the power

Of the gospel of Jesus Christ

With excellence;

Challenging Christians to

Live victoriously,

Grow spiritually,

Know God intimately.